FISHING FOR SPRING

Mary Sheepshanks

*For my brother, David Nickson,
with my love, as always*

Published by

Fighting Cock Press
45 Middlethorpe Drive
York, YO24 1NA
Editor: Pauline Kirk

Printed and bound by Culross the printers, Coupar Angus
Typesetting and layout: Pauline Kirk
Cover Design by Graham Rust
Original Fighting Cock logo by Stanley Chapman

ISBN 978-0-906744-39-0

Price £7.50

Contents

The Arnolfini Marriage

1 Shoes

Whose are the shoes she sees
out of the corner of her eye?
The pale husband, in sanctimonious hat
and fur-trimmed opulence,
looks an unlikely bet
to walk, Red Indian-style,
in someone else's moccasins –
trying their views for size
and feeling where the pinch is.

She appears skewer-stiff and oven-ready,
trussed and dressed for her new role as wife;
dutiful, perhaps, yet apprehensive too
– but at least she owns her thoughts.

On the back wall, round as a goldfish-bowl,
a looking glass reflects on life.
In front, a small dog, jauntily confident,
barks to be let out, scenting liberty beyond closed doors.
He'll be allowed to go – but what of her?

Does her green dress announce fecundity?
Is she already impregnated with his seed,
his cold inflexibility, his rule? Did he hedge bets,
only taking her as wife, once he was sure
she could deliver Arnolfini replicas
to carry on the name?

What do the kicked-off sandals
signify to her? Did she once run barefoot
through morning grass and
dance to the dawn chorus?
Will she pull out restricting pins
to feel hair streaming in the wind again
and the sun's kiss on her cheek?

Out of the corner of her eye
does she see freedom slinking past
the open window while she puts on
the shoes he chooses now.

2 After the Funeral ...
... a daughter looks back

Who would have guessed
from their wedding portrait
the way it all turned out?
My mother's eyes are lowered,
no stray lock escapes under the primness
of those nuptial drapes.
My father looks quite sober –
Dear God! What a turn up for the books!
No hint of the ale-soaked bully,
the foul-mouthed womaniser,
who caused her such distress.

Inside the frame,
the marriage looks set fair.
No signs, as yet, of gin-stained dress
and slattern's hair, the unwashed dishes,
or untended fire; the piles
of dirty washing that enflamed his ire –
that air of martyrdom I grew to dread,
worn like a second skin.

When did it all go wrong?
They'd hoped, of course that I would be a son,
heir to the merchant house of Arnolfini –
the rightful conclusion
to what they had begun on their first night,
before that wedding knot became a noose.

I shall not keep the picture –
sad reminder of might-have-beens.
Let it go now, along with the old house,
and other goods to pay the debts.
It can't be of much value –
though Van Eyck is still well thought of
so I hear ...and you never know:

some fool may buy it.

Arthington Viaduct

An ectoplasm of a morning ...

...and the viaduct looms
above the river Wharfe
to hump its arches over the haze
unsettling as a sighting
of the Loch Ness monster.

A banshee wail echoes eerily
as a ghost-train rattles
over slippery rails to be
swallowed by the tunnel's mouth
– and lost to view.

Mist is a rising sea of doubt;
questions swirl and hover ;
hide hopes; veil ancient beliefs.
When will the sun rise again
to dispel uncertainty?

August ...

...is such a surly month!
Trees droop about in dowdy dress;
herbaceous borders, stressed
by summer's haute couture,
shrug off sartorial rules
and look a mess.
Hems of delphiniums wilt,
decay is in the air:
the phlox smell musty.

Moulting birds
with feathers drab and dusty
resign from local choirs,
eschewing joie-de-vivre
like puritan John Knox –
even the finches seem
post-natally depressed.

Persistent summer rain
– once badly-needed –
outstays its welcome
like party guests
who linger on too long
after the evening's over,

Ah, but take heart! Remember –
what pleasure's on the way!
Once dead-green August's gone ...
...we get old-gold September!

Cobwebs?

A giant left his fingerprints
on every pane of my front door:
all fifteen little panes of glass
bear witness that a stranger passed
and pressed a finger on each one.
What message do these prints convey?

Did a colossus cross my lawn
with one enormous easy stride
simply to pass the time of dawn?
Perhaps the caller wished to say
'Olympian Gods have walked this way
– a sight of one is very rare:
we vanish at the break of day.'

I trace the threads from safe inside
as sunlight slants across my life
to spangle fresh ideas with light.
I see the morning through new eyes
– but wonder, awestruck, all the same
if strolling deities are tame?

My neighbours look at me askance
and are appalled that I don't care
whether the window-cleaner's been:
'That rhymester is a bad housewife,
she needs to give her place a clean –
arachnids leave a nasty stain –
where are her cloths and *Windowlene?*'

If they had heard the thrilling tread
of mystic, early-morning dance
they might have got a worse surprise –
but I am glad a giant called
to press his fingers on my door
and show me cobwebs – in disguise.

Editing

Delivering a poem
often requires the skilled assistance
of an obstetrician .

First, there's our pleased surprise
at such a rare achievement;
then rapture – the thing's so cute –
unlike anything others have produced.

Gripped by inability
to recognise its imperfections
we worship at the shrine
with star-struck gaze ...

...until we start
the long, slow haul
of bringing up the prodigy
when doubts set in:
how can we modify the little horror?

The Chinese once had a go
at editing their daughters' feet
but mercifully no longer pobble children
in an effort to improve their charms.

Funny that pruning a poem
is usually so beneficial.

Charlie-the-Chalice
(For CRBC with love and apologies)

Charlie is facing a painful dilemma
that gives him cold-sweats, palpitations and tremor
for at Mirthley, St Mungo's, the trendy new vicar
wants to rip through the Eucharist very much quicker.
He's appealed to The Vestry to find him a server
to hand round the chalice with suitable fervour
but Charlie-the-Chalice is losing his voice
at the news that The Reverend has made him top choice.
Belief will be tested, with doubts he must wrestle
at the sad lack of hygiene surrounding the vessel,
for while punters are queuing – all eager for sips –
will they besmirch the cup with their lips?
The terrible vision that's gnawing at him
is of breeding bacteria crusting the rim
 – of colds, impetigo, an unpleasant bout
of bird-flu or pink-eye, bronchitis or gout –
for he fears his immunity'd never survive a
dribble of post-Eucharistic saliva.
He's thought about straws and disposable beakers
(which didn't go well with the sacrament seekers)
he's toyed with ideas of a Germoline wipe
if the mouths of communicants look over-ripe,
but would it show piety, reverence and love
to proffer the cup in a Marigold glove?
Might the bishop agree if he ventured to ask
dispensation to serve in a surgical mask?
All his life, in October, the cry has gone up
'watch out in the winter for germs on the cup!'
and Charlie-the-Chalice would feel so much safer
if the parish converted to dunking the wafer.

Hitherto he's been pleased to belong to the 'Piskie'
but as martyrdom looms it's begun to seem risky
and Charlie's becoming as thin as a wraith
from the clinical questions eroding his faith.
Would he be healthier, feel more at home,
if he switched to his left foot and dunked off to Rome?

My Mother's Hat

Be warned, if you would pen a sonnet
in praise of homemade Easter bonnets
I know from sad experience that
faith can be shattered by a hat.

I always knew I'd lose my cool
should Mum come, hatted, to my school
and blame my spiritual defection
upon her millinery confections.

One day she did her awesome best
with green baize from the silver chest
– a hirsute hat whose monstrous brim
was fringed with bobbled lampshade trim

and draped in her bee-keeping veil.
I offered God one heartfelt wail
and prayed he'd make her stay away ...
    ...*she wore the hat on Parents' Day*!

Eucalyptus

A leaf crushed in my fingers
crumbles the years away.

I'm wrapped and smothered,
trussed in panic.
'Don't move till I come back'
she says, 'or you'll get scalded.'
A safety-pin – so called –
closes the vent to air and light
as, wreathed in steam,
I wait and wait.

Tented under a towel
with my cowardly obedience,
clogging cold and chronic fears
I sit, desperate to catch
clack of returning footsteps,
click of lifting latch
– the sounds of rescue.

Aeons later, she returns:
'Good heavens! *Silly child* –
are you still under there?
The water must have cooled down
long ago. You should have called me.'
The odour of injustice
lingers on my fingers.

Double Standard

June, and the dawn chorus tuning up
as a breeze sashays over the fields,
swinging its hips, sinuous as a sea-serpent:
it snakes ripples over the surface of the barley
whispering of secrets hidden in its depths.

Suddenly, very close, pointed receivers,
programmed to pick up a warning
of early walkers exercising dogs,
rise quivering above the sea of stalks
– hearing-ears amid the ears of corn?

Spellbound, I watch ... as cautiously
first one head, then two smaller ones
emerge to peer at me: a roe-deer mother
with twin calves. I feel privileged,
their undercover location safe with me

...then uncomfortably recall Sunday lunches:
gravy and redcurrant jelly enjoyed
with pot-roast haunch.

A Day-trip for Waxwings

A sudden murmuration, swelling loud
above the gabbling of a stream in spate:
percussion sections practising on clouds –
a timpanist's invasion of a tree?

The air vibrated with such revving sounds
it brought me rushing from inside my house
expecting vandal starlings on a raid.
But no, upon this bright October day

there was a pageant gathering at my gate –
not spivs in shades and leather biking kit
but silver-armoured medieval knights
with crests and plumes in saffron, scarlet, white.

An Icarus-of-migrants come to dine
upon the rowan berries down the lane –
a roistering band of revellers from abroad,
who feasted boisterously for several hours

then, sated, whirred away. I pray that they
won't flock too near the sun on their home flight.
Though sorbus trees may keep the witches out
I hope these cavaliers fly in again.

Mr White-Throat
'Would Like to Meet ...'

Has this neat little bachelor left it too late
to advertise for a white-throated mate
as he sings from my lilac, displays on my gate
to capture the girl of his dreams for a date?

He'll court her with dance, (blade of grass in his bill)
and his vertical song-flight should give her a thrill
as he puffs up his fawn-feathered chest to a frill,
vibrating with coloratura-like trill.

He lauds his attractions with maximum hype:
 'Spry Single Gentleman, fine treble pipe,
seeks buff-plumaged lady of similar type
for sexual adventures when timing is ripe.'

He'll feed her with larvae and offer protection,
construct sample nests for her sharp-eyed inspection
then build, with her help, a final confection
of horsehair and down for total perfection.

After travels so arduous, journey so long,
the proof of his stamina's certainly strong
– may the female he fancies agree to belong
to this miniscule troubadour, wooing with song.

Enigma

What colour peace? A deep and midnight blue –
or is it like Spring – of mingled colouring
and softer hue?
Is it in midnight flowers filled with dew
and in the feathery half-shades
of a Summer night –
hidden in that still hour
when the faint light
of stars is dimming and the mysterious sound
of running water from a moon-smooth stream
murmurs in contrast with the silent ground?

What colour joy? A young and living green –
or is elusive joy made up of many things?
Can it be seen
at early morning, when a silvery sheen
sparkles from dewy cobwebs
and an ethereal trace
of veiling mist
is draped across the face
of the fresh earth? And is joy in the flight
of swooping swallows and of building birds?
Is joy a radiant dawn and peace the night?

*('Enigma', written when I was seventeen, was published in
'The Sunday Times': my first published poem. Beginners' luck
indeed! It gave me – briefly – a very false idea of the likelihood
of future acceptances!)*

Eighteen Years

As swift as an eyelid's blink
or as long as a life sentence?
It is eighteen years
since a small grandson said
'I do miss Grandpa's big hello
don't you?' ...
Eighteen years today
since the first howl of loss
became the long low whisper
of missing you and started,
after our thirty-seven years
of close communication,
my one-way conversation
with the dead.

The Likeness – *a Ghazal*

You don't respond to praise or blame
or show surprise to read your name
                       come back to me

You can't enjoy the eulogies
in *Times* obituary acclaim
                       come back to me

No sudden laughter, glance exchanged
no muttered whisper, sharp exclaim
                       come back to me

No crosswords shared, no books discussed
with fierce dissent or thoughts the same
                       come back to me

No mountains climbed, rare species found,
no expeditions after game
                       come back to me

No trees to prune, no shrubs to plant
no brambled wilderness to tame
                       come back to me

No river walks, no season's change
– not May's glad green nor autumn's flame
                       come back to me

I touch your lips – the glass is cold –
you're locked inside a photo frame
                       come back to me

*The Ghazal: Origins in Persia – a poem in couplets – one rhyme being
carried through after the first couplet, e,g a rhyming scheme AA, BA,
CA, DA, etc. The form usually includes a refrain after each couplet
and the poem tends to be 'a cry from the heart'.*

Letter to a House

You taught me how to live alone:
grow gradually more confident
in my own company; explore
the unwanted ways of widowhood.
The emptiness
which echoed round my heart
was not of your making:
your solid, old stone walls
evoked no memories,
for he and I had never
shared your shelter.

You issued challenges
but put safe arms around me   .
after each small, but daring venture
into the wilderness territory
of solitude. Under your roof
I learnt to be the explorer
– still furbishing a cave
but learning skills
as hunter-gatherer too.

Now I am leaving you ...
... and it feels like a betrayal.

Halcyon Memories

Once their bodkin-sharp beaks,
threaded with jewel-coloured silks,
were the needles that stitched
together the days of my childhood

joining week to week and year to year
as they wove a repeating pattern, darting
through a supply of minutes that seemed, then,
as plentiful as our nursery bag of tiddlywinks.

The Thames mirrors the mystic whiteness of swans
and reflects a castle in its dungeon depths as
daydreams and willows are embroidered on the sky,
and the river's edge is silvered with minnows.

Sighting kingfishers is a rare treat now
and those shiny minutes, once flipped into the pot
with such casual prodigality, are in short supply
– but I can still unroll my halcyon tapestry.

The Road to Dunkeld

Arthur Rackham could illustrate
the tangled tree roots of these woods
but might add goblins and witches.
with cobweb hair and twiglet fingers.

Perhaps his Goose Girl,
long locks lilting in the wind,
walked bare-foot by the river Tay,
to drive a flock as white as the swans
that now beat Perthshire skies
with whirring wings?

Roe deer play at statues
and today I saw a barn-owl
– which should have been asleep –
win a territorial mind-game
with buzzards round a gargoyled oak.

What is it about this twisty road
that makes me, on routine trips
to butcher, chemist or the Co-Op,
expect the unexpected – black rabbits,
winter-white stoats, a silver fallow deer
and once, a heron waiting at a bus stop?

Next time I run out of sugar or eggs
will there be unicorns and dragons
crossing Telford's bridge?

Icebergs and Onion Skins

Nine tenths of icebergs
are submerged:
only the tip appears
above the Arctic flow
while many tiers
hide secretly below
the freezing waters.

How many layers
an onion grows
to hide its heart, and yet
it would be strange
to see a chef begin
to peel one, very gently,
skin by skin.

Onions get chopped
in chunks or finely sliced
while cooks can barely see
for all the tears they cry.
How is it then
when human hearts
are pierced
some eyes stay dry?

Autumn Leaves

I kick through fallen leaves
and stub my toe on a discarded verse.
I pick it up: is it a worthless trinket
or a valuable antique?

I still quite like its thought
but find the carving, frilly, overwrought.
Could it be modernised and made
editor-friendly, less melodic, TERSE
...or would more tinkering
only make it worse?

I take it home intent on renovation
but though I am ham-fisted, rash,
(no one has ever called me deft)
decide to go ahead and have a bash
with minimalist masterpiece in mind.

Death to all adjectives! Get rid of rhyme!
Murder tautology! Alliteration out!
A rush of power: delete! delete! delete!
superfluous syllables fall fast.

A pause for admiration:
it looks a bit bereft but still I hack away ...
to find at last...oh damn and blast! ...
the rhyme is lost, the metre's cracked,
meaning's completely gone astray ...

... there isn't any poem left!

Painting with the Winds

What colour is the wind today,
that Boreas shimmers from the north?
White and blue and shivery grey,
ice and gentians on his breath
to fan the ashes in my hearth.

Does Notus burnish southern winds
to drift bright dreams through summer trees
in opal shades of sea and sand,
gilding with sun-flower-tinted breeze
the silver-fingered olive leaves?

Bleak Eurus' eastern palette's dark
with gloomy greens as sour as bile
since Poseidon, churlish, stuck his fork
to churn the ocean's lurching swell
into a surly, heaving pool.

Zephyrus, swaggering from the west
– before whose rage leaf-armies fled –
daubs flaming orange, autumn-dressed:
Sienna browns and clashing reds
spark bonfire music in my head.

Aeolus, ruler of the winds,
can colour pictures with his voice,
transform a rainbow into sound
– old master of melody and pace
he never paints the same tune twice.

A Survey

I need to make an inventory:
try to evaluate this house,
furnished so long ago,
in which I can't remain.
The fabric's shabby now:
too threadbare to be patched again.

Can I be resolute to look
on skylights of success,
dark holes of failure
and fling the shutters back
on cobweb corners
that once made me cry?

Some doors guard secrets
best left undisturbed, but
other rooms I'll linger in
privileged to recall
what happiness I found
inside their walls.

What treasure may I pack
to comfort me
on this strange journey
I must make alone –
and how will the survey read
when the last eviction order's sent?

Requiem for Fee
For Olly, Harry and Robert

You'll find her still where curlews call
and lichened rowan trees, beside a burn,
stipple their scarlet berries on the sky.
She'll be where eagles sail and plovers cry
and red deer run. She'll come to you
where waterfalls spill elegies down tumbled stones
and white-bibbed dippers bob and dart
from rock to rock by moss and fern.
There, on the hill, you'll hear her echo ring
and glimpse her shadow pass
– unfettered now by illness –
over upland grass.

Questions haunt those who loved her so
– those whom she loved so much
yet left behind – but
viewed in the context of eternity
her final pain is but one grain of sand
upon the sunlit beach of her whole life.

Remember her for loyalty and high courage;
for friendship, fun and common sense.
Recall her femininity ... the gift she had
for making home a place of happiness
full of those family values she held dear.
Remember bubbling laughter
and the touching tears which sprang,
spontaneous, from a caring heart,
always – with her – a part
of greetings and goodbyes.

You'll sense her walking dogs
through frosted fields
or find her essence where the river flows
when winds blow green through summer trees.
Strawberries and the scent of freesias
bring bright memories back;
you'll hear again her cry of glee
at finding one more cowrie shell
by Hebridean sea;
and when you hear that very English sound
of bat on ball, you'll feel her there once more,
watching the cricket till the close of play
... and be reminded of the joys you shared.

Bare Branches

I envy winter trees
that face with dignity the chill and change
of that inevitable frost
which strips all summer camouflage away.
Trees stand as proud in winter's nakedness
as in the glamour of their garden-party dress.

Against the heartache of December sky
brave branches stretch with grace
 – no truth concealed –
wear no deceiving finery to fool the eye.
Oh leaves of youth that used to clothe me round
I fear the wind that blows you to the ground!

Ripple Effect

Some poems are like new tennis balls
served with precision at intended targets
to skim white lines at speed
and score a point.

Some verses are mere pebbles
plopped casually into a pool
with experimental toss, yet their ripples
may ring out to lap on ...and on ...

drifting grains of sand
inside our memory to lodge there,
not scoring points or winning anything
but oystering words into pearls

which sing as insistently
as the harness bells of Robert Frost's small pony,
unexpectedly stopped on its snowy journey
through the dark woods of night

with many miles still left to go ...
...with many miles to go ...

Meeting Point – *Félicité Perpétuée*
(A sonnet for Nigel and Measy   23ʳᵈ July 2007)

No pace-maker is needed for two hearts
that chime in harmony, love's magic dance
for both a second chance: that fireside art
of instant communication at a glance.

A lantern-flame's been shared for twenty years
to shine on friends and light up art and books;
two lives, once 'yours' and 'mine' becoming 'ours'
– viewpoints exchanged with just a laughing look.

One partner tends to counsel *laissez-faire*
while one, impetuous, favours hasty dash
but, balanced finely, now between the pair
ideas produce excitement, not a clash.

Noon may be past but evening skies look bright
with stars of happiness before goodnight.

A Prayer

Oh take me where the river flows and softly blows
through summer grass a secret wind. Oh let me pass
alone, away – oh let me pray
so far and quiet that I may fill
my soul with silence – and be still.

Take me to where the curlews call and water falls
with silver songs on rock and stone. Let me be strong
to be apart – hear in my heart
the warning words that we are bound
to walk with gentleness on sacred ground.

Oh let me go where torrents roar and eagles soar
on outstretched wing; catch canticles that skylarks sing
high in the sky; hear plovers cry
to windswept hills and healing space.
There in that saving silence – grant me grace.

Making Muesli for Angels

Should you ever glimpse an angel
beating its wings against
a stained-glass window
(trying to escape to a
better ventilated environment)
open the doors, go outside – and wait.

Scatter some prayers if you like
to entice it to fly in your direction
but be suspicious of proprietary brands
 – they can contain hypocrisies
which are poisonous to angels.
Why not make your own mix?

Try to offer a balanced diet:
scrutinise ingredients for freshness,
use common sense for bulk,
go easy on reverence
and always add a little laughter
to lighten the mixture.

Never store angel-mix
in the freezer or in air-tight tins:
and remember – you cannot own
an angel: they do not thrive
in captivity but should be viewed
with an open mind

and ... caution.

.

Canine Conversation

Do you fancy a Lhasa or Shiddy?
My friend's got a nice little bitch
but its coat resembles a matted old Yak
so you cannot tell which end is which.

Would you rather we purchased a Yorkie
or perhaps you'd prefer a Min-Pin?
If you long for a dog that looks dainty
shall we go for a Japanese Chin?

I've still got a yen for a Bloodhound
with wrinkles more droopy than mine
— but there isn't much room in our 'semi'
to train it to follow a line.

When our Poodle tried *Strictly Come Dancing*
the neighbours declared her a 'natch'
and our Beardie's become so obedient
he can run over seesaws and catch.

The Pom's got such bad alopecia
his hair's falling out in great tufts
and our Dandy's just eaten the postman ...
...will we ever be ready for Crufts?

I've run round the ring with the Dachsy
(our legs make us look much the same)
but my Rotty's pinned down the head steward
and the judge seems to think I'm to blame!

Treachery?

Was I a traitor when I rang the vet
to plot a murder on the telephone?
God knows I felt like one, and yet
at least she died at home and not alone.

It seemed to me a greater treachery,
to prolong her life: to watch her puzzled shame
at her incontinence, and hear her cry
at such indignity – although there was no blame.

I sat beside her on the bean-bag bed
where she had always slept. I hope she didn't know
this was the last time I would stroke her head
before she went wherever dead dogs go.

A needle in her leg: she gave no sign
of fear, just laid her nose upon my lap,
and she was gone – and all the pain was mine.
Fifteen years devotion leaves a gap.

Not Hatching Words

The tutor passed a box round: 'Take your pick.
Don't stop to look; selection must be quick –
whatever you draw out will speak to you..'
I've picked a wooden egg. No words ensue!

I wish I'd chosen something else instead
of this unyielding item – background red,
beneath unlikely flowers painted black.
Will someone notice if I slip it back?

I thought, like Russian dolls, it might divide
revealing, layer by layer, more eggs inside;
but this one's solid – won't unscrew. I ask
what hidden message could its surface mask

that I can't see? A yolk, a chick – a thought?
Are there some poems here I haven't caught?
I wait for inspiration, hope to find
that ovoid sonnets now invade my mind.

The other students' muses start dictating
while I sit, egg-bound, word-deaf, glumly waiting,
and recognize, while gazing at the clock,
my egg is just a lump of writer's block.

The Sappho of Swansea
(With acknowledgements to Miss Joan Hunter Dunn)

Mrs Lillian Bard-Jones, Mrs Lillian Bard-Jones
what powerful poems you feel in your bones!
How firmly you flex all your poetic muscles –
words pound through your blood instead of corpuscles.

Oh Mrs Bard-Jones – Swansea's own Sapphic Lillian –
odes trip from your lips by the trillion and zillion
as terror-struck neighbours accept invitations
to wine and to dine for your bardic orations.

Your lust for the lyrical never grows dimmer
(for you've been reciting from cradle to zimmer)
and what entertainment could really be finer
than you reading rhymes from your garden recliner?

You toss off pantoums, sonnets flow without stopping
(it's said you write villanelles while you're out shopping)
you're a dab with iambics, and I've got a hunch
you could knock up a rondeau while cooking the lunch.

To come to your soirées and hark to your muse
is a summons no lyricist dares to refuse;
after elderflower pressé, with sponge cake replete,
it's a very brave poet who'd dare to compete,

for, a ship in full sail on the metrical main,
you regard any rivals with scorn and disdain.
They "merely write verses" – but *you* are a poet
and Lillian Bard-Jones ...don't you jolly well know it!

A Perfect Conversation

So much courtesy!
Such listening and responding
in this finely balanced
harmony of give and take –

instant attunement
to another's rhythms
making a poetry
of understanding

like perfect sex
shared amusement
unconditional love –
Bach's Double Violin Concerto.

Karma?

I called the dogs off
as they nosed at something
on the icy doorstep –
sliding it along like a miniature curling stone.
I expected a dead shrew or frozen wren.

What was it doing late at night
 – a freezing, snow-bound
Scottish Highland night – this
tiny, living prototype for a dinosaur,
God's *Airfix* model of a crocodile?

Had it been conjured by my dreams of Greece
 – inch long reminder
of hot evenings and chilled wine;
bikinied bodies basking on a beach;
cicadas tuning Stradivarius legs?

Perhaps this worshipping of warmth
will cause my karmic self
to be reincarnated, reptile-like, upon a rock?
But it would be a nasty shock
to find myself a lizard ... in a blizzard.

The Shrine

Ancient terracotta pots
cast shadows down the Lemon Walk
as distant bells, insistent, call
hours from the campanile clock
under a blue Bellini sky.

Set in the crumbling terrace wall
a dark oak door with iron locks
creaks open to reveal inside
a Cardinal in clear glass box,
unlikely rosebuds round one eye.

Hard to believe he's lived at all,
this lolling midget, hunched and small,
a bridesmaid's garland on his head,
so rakish – but so very dead.
Massed reliquaries hang below

all neatly labelled, so we know
to whom and where our prayers should go:
there's skin off shins, a bishop's toe,
a sacred eyelash, saint's old shoe;
splinters of cross to ward off woe.

But are we less disaster prone
when clutching saintly bits of bone
or fondling threads of martyr's shrouds?
And do the angels laugh aloud
to watch the hopeful touching wood?

We surely give God cause to weep
... is he amused at what we keep?

Trespassing

Slim, gold-embossed, calf-covered,
paper translucent-thin,
musty with closed-up longing –
what memories hide within?

I trespassed through the pages
of the volume by her bed
and felt that I'd intruded
on secrets long since dead

as I found a four-leaved clover
imprisoned in the book –
was it just to mark a poem
or recall a laughing look?

Had her lover found and picked it
in the grass beside the burn?
Did she hope that if she kept it
carefree dalliance might return?

Do leaf-spells lose their magic
once green sap's been pressed away
– and only last while clover blows,
air-free, in meadow hay?

Waving Prayer-Flags

When tattered prayer-flags flutter in the breeze
to signal *Mayday* calls of love or pain
they transmit supplications from the trees.

Does God (if God exists) approve such pleas
or groan as bells and gongs boom yet again
and tattered prayer-flags flutter in the breeze?

Some suppliants pray from hassocks on their knees;
count beads; light candles; intone choral strains
– and some transmit petitions from the trees.

Are high-tech angels trained to decode these,
dispatching heaven-wards the sad refrains
from e-mailed prayer-flags fluttering in the breeze?

Round ancient certainties doubts mock and freeze.
Dare we believe a loving God remains
while prayer-flags flap unnoticed in the breeze
and screaming supplications wave from trees?

Fishing for Spring
for B with love.

A bright metallic chink of sound at dusk
as one bold blackbird's call casts out a lure
to spin for dawdling spring and reel it in.

Snowdrops, in pristine surplices, float
green Gregorian notes on moss-damp air
while bell-rope catkins ring out hedgerow chimes.

Rooks start to renovate old properties
and smoking censers puff pink prophecies
round the expectant larch trees in the woods.

Snow may yet threaten, winds flick wicked blades,
but there's a tug on February's fishing line ...
...has spring been hooked?

Invocation to a Kingfisher
For Susannah with love

Flash past me to dispel despair
and light my darkness with your beam;
pipe your bright call to challenge me
across the lake, above the stream!

Come as a rapier thrust of hope,
a lightning fork to stretch my eyes;
an alleluia shout of praise
Te Deum-feathered to surprise.

You commandeered Our Lady's cloak
from Raphael's Nativity;
seized jewelled chalice, gilded cope;
took fire and sand; Ionian sea.

Did windows shatter, once, at Chartres
so you could steal some splintered glass
– wear Joseph's coat upon your flight,
sport Noah's rainbow as you pass?

Illuminate my Book of Hours,
pen me a message with your quill;
rekindle faith to light my path
through the dark wood, up that last hill.

Acknowledgements are due to the following, in which some of these poems have appeared:

Acumen, Aireings, Artemis, The Countryman, Envoi, Farmers Weekly, Gabrielle, The Lady, Pennine Platform, Second Light, The Spectator, Yorkshire Journal, The Sunday Times.

Also By Mary Sheepshanks

Fiction
A Price for Everything
Facing the Music
Picking up the Pieces
Off-Balance
The Venetian House   (writing as Mary Nickson)
Secrets and Shadows (writing as Mary Nickson)

Non Fiction
The Bird of my Loving
(A personal response to loss and grief)

Poetry
Patterns in the Dark
Thinning Grapes
Kingfisher Days
Dancing Blues to Skylarks

Other publications available from
Fighting Cock Press

Webbed Skylights of Tall Oaks (anthology), ed. Clare Chapman	£4.00
After Passchendaele: a Writer's War, Mabel Ferrett	£6.50
Kingfisher Days, Mary Sheepshanks	£5.00
Dancing Blues to Skylarks, Mary Sheepshanks	£6.00
Thinning Grapes, Mary Sheepshanks	£6.50
Natural Light, Ian M.Emberson	£3.00
Fighting Cocks: Spirit and Emotion, Mabel Ferrett (ed. P. Kirk)	£12.50
Fighting Cocks: Mind and Body, K.E.Smith (ed. P. Kirk)	£12.50
Envying the Wild, Pauline Kirk (ed. Mabel Ferrett)	£5.95
Patterns in the Dark, Mary Sheepshanks	£6.50
Fosdyke and Me And Other Poems, John Gilham (with Stairwell Books, USA)	£6.50
Temporary Safety, Rose Drew	£6.50
Dune Fox and Other Poems 1981-2011, Colin Speakman	£3.00
Beyond the Window, Alan Gillott	£7.50

www.fightingcockpress.co.uk